T0381449

Haiku
FOR ALL SEASONS

JOSEPH R. SAPONE

WESTBOW
PRESS®
A DIVISION OF THOMAS NELSON
& ZONDERVAN

WestBow Press books may be ordered through booksellers or by contacting:

WestBow Press
A Division of Thomas Nelson & Zondervan
1663 Liberty Drive
Bloomington, IN 47403
www.westbowpress.com
844-714-3454

ISBN: 979-8-3850-0998-5 (sc)
ISBN: 979-8-3850-0999-2 (e)

Library of Congress Control Number: 2023920711

Print information available on the last page.

WestBow Press rev. date: 02/27/2024

Haiku is a Japanese form of poetry that is very short but each haiku creates a powerful image almost immediately. Most haiku celebrate nature in all of its aspects and inspire the reader to envision a world of beauty and wonder. One is always taken by surprise in the 17 syllable poem.

Joseph Sapone wrote these haiku to express his love of nature in all of the seasons, especially at Christmas time. Combining his love of nature with his Christian faith make his haiku very American in feeling. St. Frances was his favorite saint and was an inspiration for many of the haiku.

CHRISTMAS

It is in darkness
That we see a candle glow…
Blessed Christmas night.

Dec. 1997

Only in silence
Can the Holy Child come…
Be still and listen.

Dec. 1997

In the Beginning
Only the Word without Christ…
Christ, Word Incarnate.

Dec. 1996

Like Winter waiting
The coldness within our hearts
Turns to Joy this Morn.

Dec. 2002

Why the animals
To greet our Saviour's birth
On Christmas morning?

Dec. 2002

Once inside the Church...
Steam rising from our fingers
Like incense to God.

2000

An oxen breathes warmth
Upon the infant Jesus…
May I be an ox.

Dec. 2002

Loneliness and not…
Incomplete and yet complete,
Birth and yet rebirth.

2002

A light at midnight…
The Light of the World made man
Shining through darkness.

2000

Lights reflect on snow
Guiding us along our way
To the nearby church.

2000

Late evening snow
Creating a crunchy path
As we walk to mass.

2000

On Christmas morning
Raise our eyes and look about...
The Light of Lights has come.

Dec. 1998

Golden Christmas morn…
How our hearts yearn for His birth
To renew our souls.

Dec. 1999

Love came at Christmas
Heaven touched the earth and
Hope was born anew.

Dec. 1999

Humble are the skies
And lowly are the shepherds
To greet the Prince of Peace.

Dec. 1993

Christ, Sun of the earth
With all thanks we hail His Light
Rejoice all Rome this day.

Dec. 1998

The joy of Christmas
Does not fill the hearts of those
Who do not prepare.

Dec. 1998

Herald of the Word
Great forerunner of the morn
Christ, our Lord is born.

Dec. 1998

Oxen breath rising
Like incensed prayers to God
On that Holy Night.

Dec. 1997

Feed the lowly beasts...
Raise your voice in Joyous song,
Christ is born tonight.

Dec. 1997

And the word made flesh
That cold, clear Bethlehem night
To dwell among us.

Dec. 1995

Wrapped in swaddling clothes
Between an ox and an donkey
Lay the King of Peace.

Dec. 1995

O great mystery!
Sacrament most wonderful…
Born in a manger.

Dec. 1995

Advent candles burn
Reminding us to prepare
For the birth of Christ.

Dec. 2003

All good memories…
Candy, lights, toys, games, and love,
But best, the Christ Child.

2000

Sing praise to His Name
All shout joyfully to God
Proclaiming his birth.

Dec. 1994

Sneaking down the stairs
Peeking through the open door
Missed Santa again!

Dec. 1994

Silent falling snow
Whispering rising prayers
Announcing Christmas morn.

Bitter midnight cold,
The Glorious Impossible...
Born in a manger!

Dec. 1991

Endless blackened Night
Before the Son of Man...
Christ, Light of the World.

Nov. 1992

Throw down more bird feed,
Hang green garlands and Bright lights....
It is Christ's birthday.

Dec. 1991

Sparkling herald star,
Across Bethlehem's cold hills…
Leading us to Him.

Dec. 1991

Starry frozen night…
Breath like incense rising high,
From shepherds praying.

Dec. 1991

Moon when horns break off…
World wrapped in quiet hope
Awaiting son's warmth

Cold foxes barking…
Cold moon shining heatless light,
Warm ox breath on Him.

Dec. 1991

If you would listen...
You can hear Bethlehem,
A Journey of the Heart.

1990

Behold the Beauty,
Crystal cracking starry night,
The Christ child in born.

Dec. 1989

What can a kid do
Who is born in a manger?
Nothing...just save us.

1998

Winds of heaven blow,
Sweeping out our manger's dust…
Making clean His birth.

1989

Snow, one white mantle…
Mystical Body of Christ,
Enveloping all.

Christmas morning fog,
Through it came four silent deer…
Following His path.

1887

Snow-the Mystical Body of Christ-
Enveloping everyone and everything in
One white mantle.

1988

Look about and sing
In winter's white poverty
God is all giving.

1987

Eternity dwells,
Within the ancient pine bough…
Behold Bethlehem!

1986

Eternal Spirit,
A place where ancient pines grow…
Bethlehem awake.

Dec. 1985

Christmas reminds us
We were once as pure as snow...
Could we regain that?

Dec. 2004

A divine wind blows
Scattering the midnight stars
Announcing His birth.

Dec. 2004

Frozen shepherds watch
In silent adoration...
Blessed by their innocence.

Dec. 2004

Advent is the way
To prepare our hearts for Christ...
Now, come Christmas morn.

Dec. 01

The roads west, wind close...
Wrapped in the shroud of quiet,
We see God's mysteries.

Dec. 88

Smoke on the mountain tops
Rising as murmured prayers
On Christmas morning.

Dec. 01

Day after Christmas
Too late to welcome the Child
Into a cold heart.

Dec. 03

SPRING

Warm fresh
Spring rain,
Watering parched earth...
Germinating kiss.

Mar.97

Fragrant daffodil...
Enticing her lover bee
To a quiet kiss.

May 91

Christ calls forth flowers
As He did Lazarus from sleep
To show his glory.

Heralds of Spring
Proclaiming the end of death...
Renew our spirits.

Apr. 95

I intended to prune
But instead sat beneath
The orange maple.

Waking from our sleep...
We burst forth as daffodils,
Excited with Spring.

95

February blooms,
Yield sweet ume aromas...
But June brings plum rain.

Five petal ume,
First to bloom after winter,
Shows simplicity.

Cherry blossoms bloom
In Japan for just three days...
A lifelong pleasure.

Spring spills mad flowers
Lush and fragrant after rain...
I can smell the earth.

Oct. 06

Winter's frozen tears
Vanish under Spring's kind smile
Gentle morning sun.

EASTER

Shouldering His cross
He makes His way to His gift...
Payment for our sins.

03

Creator of earth
Christ Redeemer of mankind
Light of Light, our God.

99

Glorious morning...
Made new by the Son of man
Dying on the cross.

Apr. 95

On this happy day
Let the Earth rejoice and sing
Christ Lord is risen.

99

O Lord Jesus Christ
Stripped of all your garments
Dying for our sins.

99

Like voices singing
And silent wild dancing....
Our hearts behold Christ.

Oct.97

SUMMER

Torch flowers flutter...
Recalling wind blown smoke puffs
Across the tall grass.

Jan.98

Silent garden pond...
Speaking only through splashing
Orange, red and white.

Aug. 94

Suffocating heat...
Only the cicada's song
Penetrates the night.

Aug.02

Cicadas singing
Across waves of endless heat...
Seventeen year itch!

Aug.94

Catbirds and heat waves
Cicadas and thunderstorms....
Old dog looks so sad.

June 02

Paper lanterns glow...
Illuminating the night
Beneath the plum tree.

June 98

Raindrops on roses
After a quick summer rain...
Butterfly kisses

Aug. 94

A string of lanterns
Casting a starry glow through
Laced rice paper.

Apr.97

Slowly falling rain
Beating a steady tattoo
On the tin-roofed shed.

Green knife sun-catcher,
Hear that dull metallic splash?
Still water parting.

93

Moon shines through willows
Mirroring silver shadows...
Soul in clear water.

Aug. 94

Summer Kimono
Covering her nude body
Invisible veil.

June 04

Lying on my back
The clouds are my company...
On a lonely day.

Nov. 06

For those who can see
Magical twists of branches...
A world in a pot

Sept. 2000

White winged moth fights
Against the light temptation...
Tireless to the death.

Oct. 06

Roses bow their heads
During a benediction...
Of the summer rain.

August burning sun...
Why snail do you venture out
From your damp shelter?

Aug.02

A blue heron rests...
Tranquil, on a floating log,
Silence fills the calm.

Dec.2000

Stillness and quiet
Only the cicada's cry...
Through the summer heat.

Feb.02

Choir invisible...
A host of thrushes singing...
Deep in the forest.

Feb.07

Magnificent rose
My shears hesitate to cut...
Maybe one more day.

July 04

A quick summer rain
Relieving our garden's heat,
Though gone...refreshes.

90

Japanese beetles
Clustering on the rose blooms...
Consuming beauty.

July 94

Barking in the night
Too high pitched for a dog...
Fox–mating season.

June 98

Moon after the rain....
Night bathed by cool light,
We dream together.

Mar.96

Bird song through the trees...
Mystic chords of memory
Vibrate within us.

Jan. 01

A refuge from heat
Beneath shade from tall poplars..
Oh, for Autumn's chill. .

Oct.06

Dirty slimy slug
I despise your appetite
But love your slug-ness.

Sept.07

Flower to flower
Bees take life while they give life...
Tons of cucumbers.

Aug.07

Under a plum tree
Listening to the dark night
I count sky candles.

Feb.07

A gentle knocking
There, it comes again
Oh, this summer rain.

Wild Lily,
She dances freely
Among the tall swamp grass
Orange head shaking.

Feb. 01

AUTUMN

A cold wind whips up
Sending shivers down my spIne...
Aspen leaves shimmer.

Trick or Treaters come
Across pumpkin-filled fields...
A hoot owl screeches.

Oct. 94

Dancing running leaves
The rabbit turns to chase them
No -no playmate here.

Feb.99

Across wet cornfields
Trick or treaters dragging bags...
No one to fill them.

Signals of Winter...
Calling in endangered beasts,
To find a warm home.

Dec. 90

Spirit of the Wind
Blows across buffalo grass...
Making silent waves.

Dec. 90

Pumpkin skies rising
Falling leaves announcing...
Prepare–it's late.

Sentinel cornfields...
Ghostly reminders of Spring
Bowing in chill winds.

Dark red ribbons streak
Through yellowing pine needles...
Purple finch winging.

Harvest moon running
Fall behind, races ahead
Cheerful companion.

Autumn moon shining
In every black koi pond...
The moon, only one.

Apr. 93

Dear father missed,
Everywhere I turn...
The Autumn wind.

Abandoned wasps' nest
Hidden among the yew branches...
Where have they all gone?

Feb. 02

A grey rainy day
But I like it more than sun...
I am in myself.

Those sapphire skies
Slowly turning gloomy gray
Heralding Autumn.

Sept. 02

Chrysanthemums bloom
Down the rock strewn hillside...
Cascading gold.

Mar. 99

A cool Autumn wind
Trails me through the empty streets...
Following the moon.

Jan. 04

Autumn winds create
A red carpeted welcome
From dying maples.

Nov. 01

Fine rain pricks my face
And Autumn wind chills my soul...
Yet, a peacefulness.

Oct.99

Black Robe Scurrying
Through drizzling autumn streets...
To deliver God.

Nov. 9

Full Autumn moon,
Purple and red skies setting....
Why am I uneasy?

Sept. 99

Childhood dreams return
Looking at the Autumn moon
Through thinning oak trees.

Sept.2000

A slight chill at night
Signals the change of season...
Why do I feel sad?

Sept. 2000

Autumn reminds us
Of everything undone....
Cruel taskmaster.

Sept. 2000

Autumn replaces
Brilliant redden splashes
With orange harvest.

Nov. 2000

A cold wind whips up
Sending shivers down my spine,,
Aspen leaves shimmer.

Mar. 01

The path is wider
Now that the leaves have fallen...
I can see neighbors.

June 02

Cinnamon Autumn
The smell of roasting chestnuts
Conjures up my youth.

June 02

Autumn moon shining
Across pumpkin filled fields...
Silhouetted crow.

Oct. 94

Still in the night,
Branches tap my window...
Only the Fall wind.

Nov. 01

Lingering Summer
Reluctant or hibernate,
Sadly acquiesces.

Sept. 2000

A warm autumn rain
Confuses departing geese...
They remain to die.

Nov. 03

WINTER

Grey January skies...
Doubled in office windows
Through bare tree branches.

Nov. 91

Winter thunderstorms
Confuse our sense of being
Is it really Spring?

June 02

Sentinel pine row
Militarily erect...
Guarding a new snow.

Dec.91

Poor cover for birds
The bamboo creaks from the cold
Weighed down with snow.

Jan 02

Crows flying through snow
Coversing with each other
How much do we talk?

Feb.02

Stars in blue black night
Hanging like yellow lanterns...
Over mountain tops.

Feb.97

Stillness and the Moon...
Dreaming awake it visits me
Through frosted windows.

Nov. 01

Silent like the snow
Another year falls on me...
Birthdays can be sad.

Jan.02

Snow blows from the North
Causing the Titmouse to swerve,
Missing the feeder.

Snow layered on snow...
High up in the tulip tree,
A sentinel crow.

Mist shrouds your figure
Yet I see you through the trees
White-tailed visitor.

Feb.01

After heavy snow
Fallen branches block their path...
Confusing the deer.

Feb. 01

Pine branches obscure
The light from a winter moon...
I walk a lone path

Mar. 99

Sounds of crackling fire
From the weight of heavy snow....
Branches snap and break.

Feb. 01

Grass peering through snow
Grey skies laden with moisture...
Will it never end?

Sept. 99

Nature is hiding
Beneath a cold white blanket...
Will Spring expose her?

Nov.99

Snow falls silently
Covering imploring arms
Of Nature's saints.

Snow melting fields
Fly on the windowpane...
Cataract image.

Abandoned bird's nest
How sad to see the torn twigs...
We too leave our nests.

Wild rushing waters
Peeling away winter's coats...
How welcome the sound..

Croaking marble frog.
Frozen in perpetual
Protest to the moon.

Busy winter bees,
Gathering sterile honey...
Wait until the Spring.

Moon of popping trees...
Storms sweep down without warn1ng,
Lasting only hours.

Swaying frozen trees
Growling under the strain...
Then, a snapping branch.

Feb.94

The winter stillness
Remins us of God's presence...
We are not alone.

Jan.97

Leaves fill the birdbath
Sealed in winter's plastic rain
Spring's lovely fossils.

Flakes touch our faces
With unimaginable
Courtesy and charm.

Oct. 97

Sparkling in the night
Snowflakes dance beneath lampposts...
Winter fireflies.

Jan. 02

Cold dark icy night
Made warm by your presence
Flickering candle.

Lying half awake
Looking out the frosted pane
At moonlit pine trees.

Feb. 02

Chickadee eating
At ice-coated feeder...
Squirrels waiting below.

Feb. 99

Separate flakes fall...
One by one, then more, faster
Dancing dazzling white.

Oct. 97

In a snow whirlwind
Am I rising or falling?
Earth and sky are one.

Feb. 01

MUSINGS

I look at the moon...
We are not so far apart
When it wakens night.

Jan.04

Get rid of cloth bags
Let go of everything...
Then you are free.

Dec. 01

Formless and silent
It does not fade with seasons...
Tell me, what is this?

Oct. 01

Yes Summer has gone...
And all Winter's promises
Wait another year.

Sept. 06

Early Autumn morn...
Smoke rising from a cottage
Pointing to the sun.

Oct. 06

Shaggy unkempt cat
Sneezing unbalances his gait
Yet he clings to life

2000

Moonlight baths the path
Through the perfumed apple trees...
Will she walk this way?

July 94

A bare light build burns,
A mournful train whistle blows,
A dreadful motel.

2000

A hair in my nose
Oh dear, hair in my ears...
 No hair on my head.

Sept. 2000

Now it is too late
For us to waste looks and sighs
Just say I love you.

Sept. 2000

Standing with seedlings,
Like an oak in the forest
Is a good teacher.

Sept. 2000

Lost Aztec gold found...
Monarch butterflies gather;
Spilling their treasure.

Mar. 01

Energetic wren
Flitting cheerfully about
Sorting out his finds.

Feb. 07

Voice of the night wind..
You can talk of symphonies,
But none are like this.

Feb. 07

Hurrying Juncos
Scurrying madly for seeds
Before the snowstorm.

Feb.07

Evening breezes...
Voice of the wind is not heard
Through the sound of rain.

Feb.07

Silvering the path
Old year moon shining brightly
Through winter branches.

Feb.07

Hear the heart of night
Silent and yet many sounds...
Your voice calls to me.

Nov. 06

Scattered through the woods
Bird songs and tumbling blossoms....
Azaleas waning.

Nov. 06

From between twin peaks
A silver moon emerges
Lighting my pathway.

A young crow screaming
From an ole sycamore tree.
Calling to his friends.

Aug. 94

Winged-mouse rising
Soaring, darting, dipping low
Beneath oak's mantle.

Nov. 94

Whispering wind tells
Many secrets in our ears...
Making us wear muffs.

Feb.94

Black-cap chickadee
Quietly arrives to eat...
Not disturbing others.

Nov. 94

Listen quietly,
Breeze passing through pine needles...
No worldly worries.

Moon in the cold sky
Alone without company...
Makes us lonely too.

Dec. 06

Once more together
But our love is as fragile
As cherry blossoms.

Sept.07

I thought I had strength
But these constant pains weaken
What resolve I had.

Aug.07

Reading lets us go to
To places that we cannot...
Without a movement..

How they look at us!
They don't know that we can talk...
Old cat, I love you.

Sept. 2000

Broken flagstone path,
Dimly let by candlelight
Warns me how I aged.

Sept. 2000

Alert chickadees
Patiently wait their turn,
After rude Blue Jays.

Sept. 2000

Moments here and now
Happening once in our lives.
Oh...there I lost one.
OR
lchigo ichi-e

Sept. 99

Not one thing!
Like rushes swaying in the wind,
We rise, fall, rise, fall.

Sept.99

An old oak, gnarled
But strong and straight and true....
We learn from its grace.

Titmouse patiently
Waiting his turn at feeder,
While blue jays carouse.

Feb.99

Fog locks endless skies
Wind rises over vast plains
Expounding wisdom.

Oct. 01

There is no more joy
Than saying on the tomorrow
I shall complete that

Dec. 01

Silence and the moon
We talk but do no speak...
That is why we are friends.

Nov. 01

Stars in blue-black night
Hanging like yellow lanterns
Over mountain tops.

Feb.97

Solitary wren
Perched on a crooked reed
Blowing back and forth.

Feb.02

Grey mist above waves...
Stinging cold rain awakens
Dreams of summer sand.

Feb.02

The expanse of sky
Does not obstruct clouds floating....
It lets them drift free.

Sept. 01

Head like a turret...
Perched high in a beech tree
A hawk watches and waits.

Bright white moonlight .
When Spring is in its full bloom
Keeps the birds awake.

Apr. 03

Across a dark bay
Indifferent winds and waves
Take us home again.

Apr. 03

Cherry blossoms blooms,
Just long enough to make us
Long for them again.

May03

Wind battered pines
Point all their branches on way...
Snow swallows all sound.

Feb.04

We meet as strangers
Under the flowering pear
And leave as warm friends.

Jan. 04

White upturned deer tail
Zig zagging through the pine trees....
Warning her children.

Dec.03

Hurricane warning
Brings an ominous quiet...
Gentle wind and rain.

Sept 06

Planting in the rain
Soaks my boots and gives a chill...
Oh, for a green tea.

Sept. 06

Just a little drunk
Enough to tell jokes and laugh....
Than to love-making.

May.03

Afternoon napping
Disturbed by chirping sparrows...
How pleasant to awaken.

May04

Looking at herself
Combing her long auburn hair,
She wonders...Why him?

May03

Another birthday
Perhaps...one does not know yet
The day has to end.

Jan. 06

My lady of dawn
Needs no perfume or Incense,
I inhale her fragrance.

May -03

Here I am in bed
While Spring comes through my window...
Why am I hiding?

Apr. 03

Dancing white moonlight
Making patterns on my wall
Brings old memories..

Apr. 03

Stretch of old stone wall
Winding through the wilderness...
Who laid it in place?

Jan. 96

Not a sign of you,
Cold and alone in our bed...
Where are you tonight?

Aug. 95

Sitting on a branch
Watching our every move....
Jealous nightingale.

Aug.95

Lonely mountain path
Beckons me to solitude...
Following its' way.

Feb.94

A young crow screaming
From an old sycamore tree..
Calls to his friends.

Nov. 94

Black silence of night
intensifies your absence...
Oh, to hear the dawn.

July 94

Bison pound the range...
Bodies brewing cloaks of fog,
Shrouding their movement.

Jan. 94

Rising of the moon
Silhouetted in the sky
Through bamboo curtains.

Floating on the prairie
Scouring a mixed grass meadow...
A red swift fox hunts.

Dec.93

Lonely and confused
I find no consolation
Among people.

Budding bonsai sings
Every time you show it...
A different tune.

Apr. 93

Push down to the sea
Heavy green clouds of heaven...
Sky and water meet.

Stillness yet movement
Movement yet serenity...
Bonsai, God made you.

Ugly crossed branches
Where's the missing apex?
Watching for danger

Watching for danger...
High in the tulip poplar
A sentinel crow.

Down the sky, a hawk...
Lightening flash through white clouds
Made red by his beak.

                              Mar, 91

Listening to winds
Blowing through ancient pine boughs,
Answers all questions.

                              Mar. 91

What is behind us
Is the true path we travel...
Not what is ahead.

Many memories,
Like tired cherry blossoms....
Falling from my mind.

When we are sitting...
Opening the hand of thought
Resolves all conflicts.

Sept. 01

"Not one thing!"
Like rushes swaying in he wind,
We rise, fall, rise, fall.

Sept.99

Let every day be
A garden of pleasures
Blossoming in my heart.

Jan. 19,96

Long past money thoughts
Long past strong shiny white teeth...
I am what I   am.

Sept. 99

Bison roam the grass
Brewing grey cloaks of fog...
Ghostly prairie smoke.

Jan.98

A rare swift fox
Scouring a mixed grass meadow...
Floats on the prairie.

Jan.98

Stone Mason's jacket
Limp with blood and sweat and wear...
Crumpled like him.

June 95

Moon in a grey sky
Alone without company
Makes us lonely too.

Dec. 06

Yes, what is a kiss?
It binds us not together...
Only if you dream.

All this before us
Originally nothing....
It will be nothing.

Oct. 07

After I am gone
Will someone read these poems
They are all I leave.

Aug.07

Iced roses glisten
Unspeaking testimony
Of perfumed gardens.

To die is nothing
But not to see you again...
How can I stand that?

Aug.07

Dew on a grass walk...
Makes Matins seem more sacred
When said with bare feet.

Discomforting heat
Even friend Brownie the wren
Doesn't venture out.

Aug.07

Autumn ends summer...
All the trips I didn't take
Watching my bonsai

Sept. 99

That beautiful rose
I wanted to bring inside
Didn't last till dawn.

July 04

Call in all my friends
Invite all my relatives,,
What beautiful roses.

July 04

Plum petals falling
And the fast current takes them
On a wild ride.

June 04

Bats flit back and forth....
Hiding in the low bushes
A fox studies me.

June 04

Along the roadside
More beautiful flowers bloom
Than in my garden.

May 04

In the compost pile
Yesterday's blooming roses...
Still fragrant in death.

May 04

Welcome all you birds
It's the Feast of St. Francis...
Eat and sing for joy.

Oct. 02

Pulling out the weeds
Forces many decisions...
Like confessing sins.

Moonlight through the trees...
Longing for a harmony
I had never known.

Nov.07

Derisive crows scream
Demanging an offering...
Yet, I ignore them.

Oct. OS

A full harvest moon,
Orange on Halloween night
Where are the goblins?

Nov. 01

Inside out I freeze,
Any movement gives a chill....
Coming down with flu.

Oct. 05

Lying beside me
Wrapped in a blanket of love,
We dream long dreams

Feb. 02

Bats winging at night
Like barn swallows at daybreak...
Both wrongly disliked.

July 04

The mason's fingers
Bleed from pointing this stone wall,
Yet, he wears no gloves.

July 04

A peach basket rolls
Aimlessly along the street....
Old Bob watches it.

July 04

Rain blowing in sheets
Blinding my forward vision
Yet I see behind.

Sept.07

I thought he was dead
Clinging to an impatiens
But he flew away.

Sept. 07

Mother long gone now
Yet I still long to see you
If only in dreams.

Sept. 07

Sitting in a marsh
Sparkle like a night lantern….
A fisherman's hut.

Aug.07

Fly straight to the sun,
Run across mountain tops,
Squandering the Aztec secret.

Fulfilling the ancient myth;
Here is Cibola in flight,
Right before the eyes of all...
Save Cortez.

Brave and hardy birds
You sparrows defy cities
To bring the poor joy.

Feb.07

Saints and bums.
Are the Liberals Right?
De Leon, Lopez, and Dribben
Give the right an awful ribbing,
Pick a topic- anyone-
They'll have you crying before it's done,
Although the tears flow, fast and freely
The subject matter is rather mealy;
But in the end when Justice comes
We'll know the difference twixt
Saints and bums.

When I must say goodbye
I leave the sunshine to the flowers
I leave the springtime to the trees
And to the old folks,
I leave the memories of a baby upon their knees.
I leave the nighttime to the dreamer
I leave the songbirds to the blind
I leave the moon above to those in love
When I leave the world behind
When I leave the world behind